W9-DIG-025

MONEY

Budgeting

Heather Hammonds

A⁺

Smart Apple Media

This edition first published in 2006 in the United States of America by Smart Apple Media.

Smart Apple Media
2140 Howard Drive West
North Mankato
Minnesota 56003

First published in 2006 by
MACMILLAN EDUCATION AUSTRALIA PTY LTD
627 Chapel Street, South Yarra, Australia 3141

Visit our Web site at www.macmillan.com.au

Associated companies and representatives throughout the world.

Library of Congress Cataloging-in-Publication Data

Hammonds, Heather.
  Budgeting / by Heather Hammonds.
  p. cm. — (Money)
  Includes index.
  ISBN-13: 978-1-58340-782-0
  1. Finance, Personal—Juvenile literature. 2. Money—Juvenile literature. I. Title. II. Money (Smart Apple Media)

  HG179.H25475 2006
  332.024—dc22   2005057877

Edited by Miriana Dasovic
Text and cover design by Raul Diche
Page layout by Raul Diche
Photo research by Legend Images
Illustrations by Ann Likhovetsky

Printed in USA

Acknowledgments
The author wishes to thank Meredith Begg of Meric Digital for her expert advice.

The author and the publisher are grateful to the following for permission to reproduce copyright material:

Cover photograph: Girl counting coins, courtesy of Photolibrary/SuperStock; background image courtesy of Photodisc.

Adelaide Bank Ltd, p. 11; Comstock, © 2005 JupiterImages Corporation, pp. 23, 29; Coo-ee Picture Library, p. 27; Getty Images, p. 9; iStockphoto.com, pp. 17, 19; Photodisc, pp. 3, 7, 13, 15, 16, 18, 22, 26; Photolibrary/Index Stock Imagery, pp. 6, 12, 24; Photolibrary/Phototonica, pp. 4, 20; Photolibrary/Plainpicture Gmbh & Co. Kg, p. 8; Photolibrary/SuperStock, p. 28; Photos.com, p. 25; St Geoge Bank Limited, p. 10; US Treasury, p. 5.

While every care has been taken to trace and acknowledge copyright, the publisher tenders their apologies for any accidental infringement where copyright has proved untraceable. Where the attempt has been unsuccessful, the publisher welcomes information that would redress the situation.

Contents

Glossary words

When a word is printed in **bold**, you can look up its meaning in the glossary on page 31.

What is a budget?

A budget is a plan for managing money. It helps people to work out how much money they can spend each week, month or year. It also helps them work out how much money they can save.

By making a budget, people can see just how much money they have and where it all goes. They can make sure that they do not spend too much and run out of money. They can also use a budget to help them meet a special savings goal, such as buying a new skateboard or computer game.

A budget also helps to plan and save for unexpected **expenses**. Nobody knows when they might need some extra money!

Info-plus!

Some people make a budget using a notebook and pencil. Other people make a budget on a computer, using special computer programs.

Two friends prepare a budget to help them buy computer games.

Everyone needs a budget

Everyone needs a budget to help them manage their money.

Young people can use a budget to help them work out how to manage their weekly allowance. Parents can use a budget to work out how to manage the money they earn at their jobs. They may need to work out how much money they have to pay in bills each week, or how to save for things like a family vacation or a new car.

Governments also make a budget each year. Governments collect money, called **taxes**, from people and businesses in a state or country. The money is spent on **services**, such as roads, hospitals and schools. A budget helps the government work out how much money it can spend on such services.

The Secretary of the Treasury is responsible for preparing the budget for the government of the United States.

Info-plus!

Schools also make budgets. Money is given to schools by the government each year for school programs, library books, and many other things. A budget helps schools work out how best to spend that money.

Earning money

Everyone uses money to pay for things. There are always bills to pay and food to buy. Some people may have borrowed money to buy a house or car, and they will have to pay that money back.

Sometimes, people are given money as a gift, on birthdays or at Christmas. Most of the time, they have to earn money by working for it.

Money that people earn or are given is called **income**. Money that people spend is called an expense.

Receiving an allowance

Many young people get an allowance from their parents each week, to help them buy the things they need or want. They usually earn their allowance by doing chores around the house, or by helping their parents in some other way.

Info-plus!

Some older students have a **part-time job** after school. A part-time job is a good way of earning extra money!

A part-time job delivering newspapers is a good way to earn money.

Going to work

After they finish studying at school or college, most people get a **full-time job** to earn money. They may work for a big company with many employees, or in a small business with just a few employees. Some people may own their own business and earn money from working in that business.

Using money to earn money

It is also possible to **invest** money. There are several ways of investing money. One of the most popular ways is to put money into a savings account at a bank. **Interest** is earned on the money in the savings account.

This woman works full time as a chef in a café.

Money can also be invested to buy **shares** in a business. When the business makes money, part of that money is paid to people who own shares, called shareholders.

Info-plus!

Some governments give a special allowance to certain people, to help them pay for their living expenses.

Spending money

Spending money is easier than earning it. People need to keep track of how much money they spend each week, so that they do not spend more than they can afford. Making a budget helps them do this. It shows people how much they can afford to spend, and allows them to see where they can cut down or increase their spending. If people lose track of how much money they spend, they may run out of money!

Checking prices helps shoppers to buy items that they can afford.

Info-plus!

People should always keep receipts for the **products** they buy, to help them work out how they have spent their money. Receipts are also needed to return faulty products for repairs, or to exchange them for other products.

Cash, card, or check

Using coins or bills is one way to spend money, but there are also other ways.

Many people keep their money in a bank account. They have a plastic banking card, called a debit card, which is linked to their bank account. They use the card to pay bills and buy products. Money is taken from their bank account electronically to pay for the things they buy. Each time they use the card, they spend money from their bank account.

Some people also pay bills and buy products with personal **checks**. The checks are linked to their bank account. Money is taken out of this bank account when the person who receives the check takes it to their own bank.

Cash, banking cards, and checks can be used to pay for goods.

Debt

Sometimes people borrow money when they want to buy something and cannot afford it at the time. They pay the money back over time, with interest. This borrowed money is called **debt**. Borrowing money can be very useful, but it can also be dangerous. The borrower must be careful not to borrow more than they can afford to pay back.

Bank loans

Many people borrow money from a bank. This is called a bank loan. Banks give loans for many different things, such as houses, cars, or vacations. People who borrow money from the bank make an agreement with the bank to pay the money back. They also have to pay interest on the loan, as payment for using the bank's money.

Other **financial institutions** also lend money. Some of them charge higher rates of interest than others.

Buying your
first home

st.george

Info-plus!

People cannot borrow money from a bank or other financial institution until they are 18 years old.

This information booklet from a bank explains how customers can borrow money to buy a home.

Credit cards

Credit cards allow people to borrow money to buy something. Banks or other financial institutions lend the cardholder money. The cardholder must then repay the money, with interest, in return for using the money. A high rate of interest is often charged on money borrowed this way.

Managing debt

When a person borrows money, the amount that must be repaid each week or month should be included in their budget. If money is not paid back on time, it often attracts more interest. What began as a small amount borrowed can turn into a large amount owed, if the money is not paid back regularly.

Account Name
Mr John Smith

123456-123456

Mr John Smith
1 Example Street
New York NY 10018

Credit Limit	Available Credit
$232,000.00	$0.00
Annual % Rate	Daily % Rate
7.500	0.020547

How to Pay

Home Banking Services
Payments can be made by way of Internet or Express Line (Phone Banking). Contact the above phone number for details.

BPAY
Biller Code: 9999
Ref: 999 999 9999

Telephone & Internet Banking - BPAY
Contact your bank, credit union or building society to make this payment from your cheque, savings or credit card account. More info: www.bpay.com.au

Payment in Person   giroPOST
Please present this account intact with your payment and card to any Adelaide Bank Branch or Post Office with a giroPost sign.

Payment by Mail
Tear off this slip and mail with a cheque made payable to:
Adelaide Bank, GPO Box 1048, ADELAIDE SA 5001.

Statement	from	06 June 2005
	to	05 July 2005
Statement Number		001
Customer Number		9999999999 RC01
BSB - Account Number		610 - 101 9999999999

Page 1 of 4

Overdue Payments
Amount Due Immediately → **$1,373.00**
+

Overlimit Amount
Amount Due Immediately → **$134.76**
If outstanding 1 month or more, you will incur an arrears administration fee of $35.00.
+

Regular Payments
Minimum Payment Due **$1,471.84**

Date Minimum Due **5 August 2005**

Summary
Opening Balance	$232,006.92-
Total Credits	$1,344.00
Total Debits	$1,471.84
Closing Balance	**$232,134.76**

Payment Record
Date Paid	
Amount Paid	$

Payment Slip

Customer Number	9999999999 RC01
Date Due	05 August 2005
Date Paid	
Amount Paid	$

This credit-card statement shows that the customer owes $232,134.76, and must pay at least $1471.84 of it by the due date.

Info-plus!

Sometimes, people have several different loans. Some loans charge more interest than others. It is possible to save money by taking out one big loan with a lower interest rate. The money from this large loan is then used to repay all the other loans. This is called debt consolidation.

Needs and wants

When people make a budget, one of the first things they should do is identify their needs and wants. Needs are the things that people have to pay for each week. Wants are the things they would like to buy, if there is any money left.

Example **Zac's needs and wants**

Zac gets a weekly allowance. He uses it to pay for his karate lessons and other things that he wants.

Needs
- karate lessons
- karate equipment
- entry fees to karate competitions
- gifts for family and friends

Wants
- karate magazines
- computer games
- treats such as candy and ice creams

Zac puts his karate magazines into his "wants" column because they are not essential, like his lessons and equipment. He can buy the magazines only if he has any money left after he has paid for his needs.

More expenses

Older people usually have more needs in their budget than younger people, because they have more expenses to pay.

Example **Zac's mother's needs and wants**

Zac's mother works in an office and earns a weekly wage. Her budget is very different from Zac's budget.

Needs

- food for myself and Zac
- clothes for myself and Zac
- rent on our apartment
- electricity, gas, and telephone bills
- other bills, such as car repairs
- Zac's allowance

Wants

- a vacation
- a new car
- a new stereo system

Zac's mother decides to **prioritize** her wants. She wants a vacation most, so she will save for a vacation first, after paying for her needs. Once she has saved for a vacation, she will then save for a new car.

Setting savings goals

When people use their budget to identify their needs and wants, they can then set some savings goals. Setting savings goals will help them to save for the more expensive wants on their list. Goals give people something to aim for. They encourage people to save rather than spend the money left after they have paid for their needs.

Example — **Setting a savings goal**

You want to buy the latest CD from your favorite pop star. The CD costs $20. You make it your goal to save $2 a week for 10 weeks. You include this as savings when you make your budget. At the end of 10 weeks, you will have enough money to buy the CD.

Savings goals allow people to buy the things they need and want.

Remember that the more you spend each week on things such as candy, the less you will have to save for those special wants, like CDs.

Short-term and long-term savings goals

Sometimes people want to buy some things sooner than other things. Then it is a good idea to set both short-term savings goals and long-term savings goals.

Example

Caitlin's savings goals

Zac's friend Caitlin loves inline skating. She wants to buy some new kneepads, as her old ones have worn out. She also wants to buy some new inline skates, even though the ones she has work well. The kneepads cost $20 and the inline skates cost $100.

4 WEEKS × $5 = $20

20 WEEKS × $5 = $100

Info-plus!

When making a budget, it is important to set savings goals that you know you can meet. This helps make saving fun.

Caitlin works out that she can buy the kneepads in four weeks if she saves $5 a week. This is her short-term savings goal. However, it will take her 20 weeks to save for new inline skates. This is her long-term savings goal. She decides to save for the kneepads first, because she needs them the most.

Making budgets

Making a budget is not as hard as it seems. It is simply a matter of collecting information about income, expenses, needs, wants, and savings goals.

Example

Caitlin's weekly budget

Caitlin wants to make a budget to help her save for her inline skating equipment. She gets an allowance each week, and also earns extra money by walking her neighbor's dog every day.

The first thing Caitlin must do is work out her needs and wants.

Needs
- inline skating lesson money (one lesson per week)
- gifts (birthdays, Christmas presents, etc.)

Wants
- new kneepads
- new inline skates
- entertainment (movies with friends, CDs, etc.)
- food (extras from school cafeteria)

Caitlin's expenses can be divided into two types, fixed expenses and variable expenses. Fixed expenses are set amounts of money that are paid each week or month, such as Caitlin's inline skating lesson money. Variable expenses change from week to week or month to month, such as Caitlin's entertainment money.

When Caitlin has worked out her needs and wants, she then prepares her weekly budget as shown below.

Caitlin's weekly budget

Income

Allowance	$10.00
Dog-walking wages	$20.00
Total weekly income	**$30.00**

Fixed expenses

Inline skating lesson	$5.00
Savings	$5.00

Variable expenses

Gifts	$5.00
Entertainment	$10.00
Food	$5.00
Total weekly expenses	**$30.00**

If Caitlin sticks to her budget, her weekly expenses will be the same as her weekly income.

Caitlin lists her savings as fixed expenses, because she intends to save the same amount each week. She keeps her savings in a piggy bank. She also keeps money for her different expenses in a set of labeled envelopes.

Caitlin sometimes gets money as gifts from her grandparents. She keeps some of this money in an envelope labeled "emergencies." Then she can use it if she needs to, instead of using money set aside for other things. She puts the rest of the gift money into her piggy bank.

Tamara's weekly budget

Caitlin's sister Tamara has a full-time job, but she always runs out of money at the end of each week. Tamara has borrowed money from her parents, and also has a credit-card debt. She wants to make a budget to help her get out of debt.

The first thing Tamara must do is work out her needs and wants.

Needs

- rent (weekly board to parents, including share of food and other household bills)
- mobile telephone
- transport (weekly train ticket)
- food (lunches)
- clothing
- debts (parents $100, credit-card debt $1000)
- gifts

Wants

- entertainment
- car

Info-plus!

Some loans calculate compound interest monthly, as in this example. Others calculate compound interest daily and cost even more.

Tamara pays compound interest on her credit-card debt. This means that if she owes $1000 at 20% per year interest in January, her credit-card bill is $1000 plus one month's interest of $16.66 ($1000 × 20 ÷ 100 ÷ 12). If she pays nothing back, then she must pay 20% interest on $1016.66 in February, and so on. If Tamara had repaid nothing by the end of the year she would owe $1219.39!

When Tamara has worked out her needs and wants, she prepares her weekly budget as shown below.

Tamara's weekly budget

Income

Wages (after paying tax)	$400.00	
Total weekly income		$400.00

Fixed expenses

Rent	$80.00
Mobile telephone	$30.00
Transport	$50.00
Credit-card debt (including interest)	$100.00
Loan from parents	$20.00
Savings	$0.00

Variable expenses

Food	$40.00	
Clothing	$20.00	
Gifts	$20.00	
Entertainment	$40.00	
Total weekly expenses		**$400.00**

Tamara loves to buy new clothes and go to the movies. However, she can allow only a small amount of money in her weekly budget for clothing and entertainment. This will change when her debts are repaid. Then she can make a new budget and set aside more money for movies and clothes, as well as savings.

Like Caitlin, Tamara sometimes gets extra money as gifts from her grandparents. When this happens, she will use it to reduce her credit-card debt. She will save money by doing this, because she will be paying less interest on her debt.

19

Tips on saving

When you have set your savings goals and made a budget, it is then time to start saving that money. Sticking to your budget and meeting your savings goals can seem hard. You may be tempted to spend more on an extra trip to the movies or on a new magazine. If you resist doing this, you will reach your goals more quickly.

It is a good idea to rethink your savings goals every few weeks. Your goals may change, and you may not want that new CD or pair of inline skates any more. If your goals change, you can work out how long it will take you to save for something else instead.

Info-plus!

Everyone has unexpected expenses, where they have to spend more money on their needs than they usually do. Try to allow for unexpected expenses when you make your budget, as Caitlin did, by keeping some money for emergencies.

Young people start learning to save money with only a small amount of money.

Handy hints

Here are some handy hints to help you stick to your budget and reach your savings goals.

Use your budget to sort out any money you get as soon as you receive it. This will help you avoid accidentally spending money meant for savings.

Divide your money and keep it in separate jars or envelopes. Write a different expense on each jar or envelope.

Stick a picture of your savings goal to your piggy bank or bank book, to remind you of why you are saving.

Write your savings goal on a card and keep it in your wallet or purse. You will see it every time you spend money, and be less likely to spend too much.

Info-plus!

Get used to making a budget and saving money regularly when you are young. You will find it easier to save for big goals, such as a car or house, when you are older!

Opening a bank account

You can open a bank account to help you manage your money and reach your savings goals. If your money is in a bank account, it is not as easy to spend as the money you keep in a piggy bank in your bedroom!

Savings accounts

Most banks have savings accounts especially for young people. Choose the savings account that suits your savings goals. Some accounts pay more interest, but you must leave the money in the account for several months. Use this type of account to save for long-term goals.

Other savings accounts pay less interest, but allow you to take your money out at any time. These accounts are best for saving for short-term goals.

This girl does her banking with the help of her mother.

Info-plus!

Some schools provide a school-banking service through a local bank. Students can open a savings account and do their banking at school each week.

Checking accounts

Checking accounts are for everyday use. You can **deposit** your allowance or money from other sources into a checking account. Then you can **withdraw** your money by using a debit card at an **automatic teller machine**, or **ATM**, by visiting a bank, by telephone, or by using the Internet.

Checking accounts are useful because you do not need to carry cash around when buying things. You receive a bank statement in the mail each month. This shows how much money you have deposited and how much you have withdrawn.

Most checking accounts allow you to view your account on the Internet, to see how much you are spending each week or month.

You can check your checking account on the Internet.

Info-plus!

Bank accounts usually charge bank fees when a customer uses their account. However, most savings accounts for students do not charge bank fees.

Money-saving ideas

When you or your parents are on a tight budget and do not have much money left at the end of each week, it is important to save money wherever you can.

Saving money around the home

You can save money at home in many ways:

- Save electricity by turning off lights when nobody is in the room, or turning off the television if nobody is watching it
- Save power by putting on an extra jumper when it is cold, rather than turning up the heater
- Keep a money jar beside your telephone and pay for calls to friends out of your entertainment allowance. When the telephone bill comes, you will already have some money saved towards it

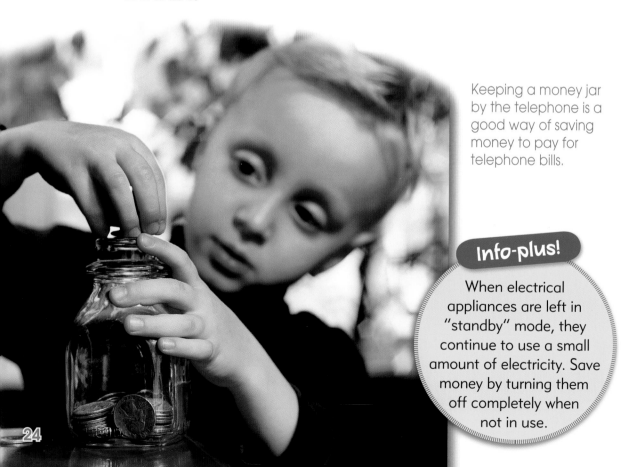

Keeping a money jar by the telephone is a good way of saving money to pay for telephone bills.

Info-plus!

When electrical appliances are left in "standby" mode, they continue to use a small amount of electricity. Save money by turning them off completely when not in use.

Saving money in other ways

There are many other ways to save money:

- Buying your lunch each day at school or work can be expensive. If you make your own lunch, you can cut your lunch costs in half

- How much money do you spend on little luxuries such as magazines, candy, and other junk food? Lots of small purchases quickly add up. Stop buying one or two of these items and you will save several dollars a week

- Do not make **impulse purchases**. If you see something you want to buy when out shopping, think carefully before buying it. Do you really need it right now? Would it be better to save your money?

Bringing lunch to school from home is a way of saving money.

Bargain-hunting

You can save money and help stick to your budget by bargain-hunting.

Supermarkets

There are many bargains at your local supermarket. Most supermarkets have their own "home brand." Instead of buying popular brand-name foods, try home brands. They cost less and are generally just as good.

Look out for weekly specials and buy them wherever possible. Supermarkets put out catalogs of weekly specials, so check them before you buy your favorite foods.

Markets

Fresh-produce markets are good places to buy fresh meat, fruit, vegetables, and other foods. They are often cheaper here than at supermarkets.

Info-plus!

Many countries have **consumer groups** or associations that put out magazines advising which products are the best value for money. You can find most of these groups on the Internet.

Fruit and vegetables are sometimes cheaper at fresh-produce markets.

Clothes

You can make big savings when shopping for clothes and shoes. Wait for end-of-season sales before buying them. They are often much cheaper, because stores are trying to clear their shelves for the new season's clothes.

Brand-name clothes and shoes can cost much more than items that look similar but are made by another company. Brand-name items may be fashionable, but when you are budgeting it is better to save money and buy the cheaper brands.

Comparing prices

Always compare prices when shopping, especially when shopping for expensive items. Ring or visit different stores to see which store will offer you the best price for the item you want to buy.

Info-plus!

Some newspapers and Internet Web sites advertise second-hand bargains. Ask an adult to help you check them out, especially if you want to buy sports equipment or toys.

You can save money by buying clothes and shoes only during sales.

Super-savers

If you have difficulty managing your money and find it hard
to stick to your budget, you can ask a "super-saver" for help.
Super-savers are people who manage their money successfully
and reach their savings goals.

Family and friends

You probably know someone who is very good at managing their
money. They may be an older brother or sister, a parent, or other
family member. They may even be a close friend. Ask them to
help you plan your budget.

When discussing your budget, ask your super-saver
these questions:

- How do they make their budget, and can you see an example?
- How often do they change their budget and set new
  savings goals?
- What tips do they have to avoid spending too much?
- Do they have any tips for bargain-hunting?

Info-plus!

Ask your
super-saver to
help you work out
your needs and
wants.

A father helps
his daughter
to plan her first
budget.

Professional super-savers

Financial planners are professional super-savers who help other people to manage their money. Many financial planners work for banks, **building societies**, and other financial institutions.

Financial planners can:

- help their customers work out their needs, wants and savings goals
- make a budget for their customers, taking into account how much money they earn and how many debts they have
- find the best ways for their customers to invest their money
- give advice on special needs, such as saving for **retirement** or paying off debts

Financial planners must have a special licence, to allow them to advise people on how to manage their money. They study to gain their licence.

A financial planner helps people to manage their money.

Info-plus!

Some financial planners work for charities or government agencies. They help people who have very little money and have trouble paying for their needs. They also help people who have a lot of debt.

Make your own budget

Here's how to make your own budget!

You will need:

- an exercise book
- a pencil and an eraser
- a ruler
- a calculator

What to do:

1 Write your needs and wants in your exercise book. List them in order of importance.
2 Identify your short-term and long-term savings goals, and write them underneath your needs and wants.
3 Rule up a new page for your weekly budget.
4 Write your income and expenses on the budget page.
5 Use the calculator to subtract your total expenses from your income.

Info-plus!

If you have a computer, you can make your budget on it and then print the budget out.

NEEDS

WANTS

INCOME

	$0.00
Total weekly income	$0.00

FIXED EXPENSES

	$0.00
	$0.00
Gifts	$0.00
Savings	$0.00

Variable EXPENSES

Entertainment	$0.00
	$0.00
	$0.00
Total weekly expenses	$0.00

Glossary

automatic teller machine or ATM a machine used by customers with a banking card, to withdraw money or do other banking

building societies financial institutions that help their members buy their own homes by lending them money

checks printed forms used instead of cash, with instructions telling a bank who and how much to pay

consumer groups groups or associations that represent shoppers

debt money owed

deposit to put money into a bank account, or an amount put into a bank account

expenses money spent on things such as bills

financial institutions businesses, such as banks, that make money by dealing in money

full-time job a job worked regularly for the normal number of working hours each day or week

impulse purchases goods bought without any thought given to the purchase beforehand

income money received, such as weekly wages or an allowance

interest money paid to a bank account-holder for using their money, or money charged to a borrower

invest to put money into a financial institution or other business, in order to make more money from it

part-time job a job worked regularly for part of the normal number of working hours each day or week

prioritize to place in order of importance

products objects that are bought, sold, or bartered

retirement a time when a person is no longer working at a job, usually because they have grown older

services work that people pay others to do or provide

shares small parts of a company that can be bought and sold

taxes money that people and businesses pay to a government so that it can run the country

withdraw to take money out of a bank account

Index